Michelangelo

AND HIS TIMES

Véronique Milande
Art direction by Alain Lachartre

A Henry Holt Reference Book
Henry Holt and Company
New York

A PICTURE IS WORTH A THOUSAND WORDS

Xun Zi (313-238 B.C.)

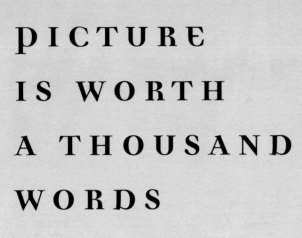

Library of Congress Cataloging-in-Publication Data
Milande, Véronique
[Michel Ange et son temps. English]
Michelangelo and his times.
p. cm.
—(W5 (who, what, where, when, and why) series)
(A Henry Holt Reference Book)
Includes bibliographical references and index.
1. Michelangelo Buonarroti, 1475–1564—Criticism and
interpretation. 2. Renaissance—Italy—Florence.
I. Series. II. Series: A Henry Holt reference book.
N6923.B9M56613   1996   95-42046
709'.2—dc20   CIP
ISBN 0-8050-4660-7

Henry Holt books are available for special
promotions and premiums.
For details contact: Director, Special Markets.

Originally published in France in 1996 by
Editions Mango under the title *Michel Ange et Son Temps*.

First published in the United States in 1996 by
Henry Holt and Company, Inc.

First American Edition—1996

Art direction by Alain Lachartre
Idea and series by Dominique Gaussen
American English translation by
Hilary Davies and George Wen
Typesetting by Jay Hyams and Christopher Hyams Hart

Printed in France
All first editions are printed on acid-free paper.∞

1 2 3 4 5 6 7 8 9 10

WORDS BY MICHELANGELO,

I KEEP A BUMBLEBEE INSIDE A JUG,

INSIDE A LEATHER BAG SOME BONES AND STRING

AND IN A VIAL THREE BALLS OF TAR

MY BLUE EYES ARE RINGED IN BLACK,

MY TEETH ARE LIKE THE KEYS ON AN INSTRUMENT

THAT WHEN THEY MOVE MAKE MY VOICE SOUND OR CEASE.

MY FACE IS MORE THAN ENOUGH TO TERRIFY;

AND MY CLOTHES WOULD SCARE CROWS FROM A FIELD

OF NEW-LAID SEED AND AWAY INTO THE RAIN

MICHELÀNGELO

Michelangelo Buonarroti gave this caustic description of himself in a poem he wrote at the age of seventy. Born on March 6, 1475, he died on February 18, 1564: eighty-nine years of passionate life dedicated to art. As his biographer Condivi noted, his horoscope proved accurate, for he was born with "Mercury and Venus in the second house, the house ruled by Jupiter, and with benign aspect, promising a noble and lofty genius, destined to succeed universally in any undertaking, but principally in the arts." He possessed all the attributes of genius—he is often referred to as "the divine Michelangelo"—but he was not handsome, the result of an incident that happened when he was a teenager. The sculptor Pietro Torrigiano tells the story: "Buonarroti had the bad habit of making fun of anyone else who was drawing there, and one day he provoked me

PICTURE BY VOLTERRA

"He has always had good color in his face. The shape of that part of his head which shows frontally is rounded so that above the ears it forms a half circle."

"The eyebrows are scanty, the eyes might be called rather small, horn colored but changeable, with little flecks of yellow and blue."

"The forehead seen from the front is square, the nose a bit flattened [but] proportionate to the forehead and to the rest of the face."

"His temples project somewhat beyond his ears and his ears beyond his cheeks and the latter beyond the rest of his face, so that his head in proportion to the rest of his face can only be called large."

"His lips are thin, but the lower one is slightly thicker so that seen in profile it projects a little. His chin goes well with the rest of his features."

"The hair is black and likewise the beard, except that, at his age of seventy-nine years, the hairs are plentifully streaked with white. The beard is forked, between four and five fingers long, and not very thick."

so much that I lost my temper more than usual, and, clenching my fist, gave him such a punch on the nose that I felt the bone and cartilage crush like a cracker. So that fellow will carry my signature until he dies." This celebrated episode has often been used to explain why Michelangelo, with his broken nose, always looked so sad and why he labored so intensely in his art to find a way of revealing the ideal beauty that fate had denied him.

This portrait was done by Daniele da Volterra around 1553; the words accompanying it are by Ascanio Condivi, biographer and friend of Michelangelo.

LOUIS XII
KING OF FRANCE (1462-1515)

The Italian Wars begin when Charles VIII of France invades Italy and seizes Naples. But then he's forced to retreat. France's next king is Louis XII, who dives back into Italy, conquering both Milan and Genoa. He forms an alliance with Spain's Ferdinand II to conquer Naples, but then gets into a war with Spain. He joins the League of Cambrai against Venice, but afterward finds himself facing the Swiss soldiers of the pope's Holy League. He starts thinking about making a truce with all his enemies.

LEONARDO LOREDAN
DOGE OF VENICE (1438-1521)

The doge allies himself with Louis XII in order to increase Venice's territory at the expense of Milan. Then he seizes some of the Church's lands and finds himself in conflict not just with Pope Julius II but with the entire League of Cambrai, which includes his former friend Louis XII, Ferdinand II of Spain, Holy Roman Emperor Maximilian I, Mantua, Ferrara, and Savoy. The league ends Venice's expansion on the Italian mainland. Venice then gets even with France by joining the Holy League.

Republic of Venice

Papal

Repub

Duchy of Milan

Republic of Flore

Duchy of Savoy

Republic of

A
v R

At the beginning of the sixteenth century, Italy is economically strong but politically weak, with a patchwork of small independent states competing for power. Its commerce and industry,—glass from Venice, silk from Milan, ceramics from Faenza, cloth from Florence—as well as its artistic and cultural preeminence make Italy an object of admiration and envy. Within the country, various rival states seek to increase their power, often by making foreign alliances: their efforts and those of other European powers to control the small states of Italy lead to the Italian Wars. The republic of Venice extends beyond the Adriatic Sea and into the eastern Mediterranean. Its prosperity threatened by the Turks, Venice seeks to strengthen its territorial claims on the mainland and as a result becomes involved in the Italian Wars. The duchy of Milan is economically prosperous and densely populated. It has been ruled by the Sforza family since 1450. Their court in Milan

EVERYONE WANTS A SHARE

Kingdom of Naples

Siena

tes

noa

FERDINAND II
A.K.A. FERDINAND THE CATHOLIC
KING OF ARAGON AND CASTILE
(1452-1516)

In 1492, Ferdinand II drives the Moors out of Granada, thus unifying Spain (and that same year he and his wife, Isabella, send Columbus on his trip). Ferdinand already owns Sicily (his father gave it to him), but he wants to extend his rule over southern Italy, which means dealing with Louis XII. His armies conquer Naples in 1504. Ferdinand also joins both the League of Cambrai against Venice and the Holy League against France.

POPE JULIUS II (1443-1513)

The pontiff wants to restore the political power of the Church in Italy. To achieve that goal, he first allies himself with France in order to take Perugia and Bologna. Later, thanks to the League of Cambrai, he recovers territories taken by Venice. The pope and Louis XII then become enemies, and the pope decides to throw the French out of Italy. To do so, he forms the Holy League, which includes Ferdinand II, Henry VIII of England, Holy Roman Emperor Maximilian I, and the Swiss cantons. (The Swiss do most of the fighting.) Just when the French have been routed, Julius dies and the league falls apart.

is brilliant and refined. The republic of Florence, artistic center of Italy in the fifteenth century and a business and banking powerhouse, is in a period of steady economic growth at the beginning of the sixteenth century. The Papal States are governed by the pope in Rome. As monarch and "warrior pope," he seeks to consolidate and enlarge his territory. As the spiritual leader of the Western Church he tries to impose his moral authority on foreign rulers. The kingdom of Naples has been ruled by the French royal house of Anjou since the thirteenth century, but the Spanish house of Aragon claims it, too, and since 1443 the kingdom has been in the hands of Alfonso of Aragon. But the French haven't given up their claim, and their dispute with Spain will help fire up the Italian Wars.

A DUNCE IN LATIN,
BUT A GENIUS IN DRAWING

The second son of Lodovico Buonarroti, Michelangelo is born on March 6, 1475, in Caprese, a tiny village near Arezzo where his father is serving a term as mayor (*podestà*). A short time later, the family moves back to Florence, and Michelangelo stays in the neighboring town of Settignano. Three more sons are born to the Buonarrotis before Michelangelo's mother, Francesca, dies in 1481.

When Michelangelo is ten, his father, hoping that his son will become a man of letters, sends him to study in Florence with Francesco da Urbino. During his three years at school, Michelangelo learns to read and write and studies Latin and Greek. But his mind is on art, and he constantly runs off to draw. He makes friends with a number of young artist apprentices, including Francesco Granacci, who is the pupil of the well-known painter Domenico Ghirlandaio. Granacci encourages his friend's budding talent by giving him sketches to copy and even talks him into considering an apprenticeship with Ghirlandaio. But Michelangelo's father is dead set against his son dropping out of school to become an artist. In the end, however, Michelangelo gets his way, and on April 1, 1488, he becomes an apprentice in Ghirlandaio's workshop with a three-year contract to learn the art of painting.

Thoroughly dedicated to his apprenticeship, Michelangelo soon gains a reputation as a skilled copyist, as the following anecdote told by his biographer Condivi informs us: "Having been given a head to copy, he rendered it so precisely that, when he returned the copy to the owner in place of the original, at first the owner did not detect the deception, but discovered it only when the boy was telling a friend of his and laughing about it. Many wanted to compare the two, and they found no difference because, apart from the perfection of the copy, Michelangelo had used smoke to make it seem as old as the original."

The influence of Michelangelo's teacher, Ghirlandaio, is especially noticeable in the strong physical energy revealed in his human forms.

Since the beginning of the fifteenth century Florence has been the center of Renaissance cultural and artistic life. Guilds, religious communities, rich merchant families, and the city itself are constantly commissioning new and exciting works of art. Over a period of 150 years nearly every major building has been built, rebuilt, or finished and decorated. There is a never-ending supply of construction sites and artworks-in-progress to explore. They provide the young Michelangelo with a fantastic education. In 1490 Michelangelo is fifteen years old and living in Florence. This is what he sees during his daily treks through the burgeoning city.

CHURCH OF SANTA MARIA NOVELLA

Work on this church began in the thirteenth century and continued for well over a hundred years. The facade was added from 1456 to 1470 by the architect Leon Battista Alberti, who advocated the use of simple geometric shapes in architecture. Michelangelo admires the uncompromising nature of Alberti's artistic style.

SOLOMON'S TEMPLE BAPTISTERY DOOR PANEL BY LORENZO GHIBERTI

This ancient church originally had wooden doors, but these were replaced in the fourteenth and fifteenth centuries by bronze doors. Andrea Pisano completed a pair of bronze doors for the south portal between 1328 and 1338. From 1403 to 1424 Lorenzo Ghiberti made doors for the north portal, after which he made another set of doors (1425 to 1452), which become even more famous and which the awestruck Michelangelo dubs the "gates of Paradise." The name sticks.

THE EXPULSION OF ADAM AND EVE FRESCO IN THE BRANCACCI CHAPEL CHURCH OF SANTA MARIA DEL CARMINE

The project for the Brancacci Chapel frescoes was entrusted to Masolino and his young and talented pupil Masaccio in 1426. It becomes the habit for apprentices in Florentine workshops to make copies of the scenes, for their realistic and moving figures are a radical departure in style from the earlier Gothic tradition.

THE BATTLE OF SAN ROMANO BY PAOLO UCCELLO

To adorn his palace, Cosimo de' Medici commissioned Paolo Uccello in 1456 to make three panels depicting the Florentine victory over the troops of Siena at San Romano. Michelangelo has the opportunity to see this astounding work while staying with the Medici, and he immediately grasps Uccello's use of line, perspective, and volume.

FIRENZE

Santa Maria Novella

Palazzo Medici-Ricca

ARNO

Santa Maria del Carmine

MICHELANGELO

CATHEDRAL OF SANTA MARIA DEL FIORE (DUOMO)
Under construction for more than a century, the Cathedral of Santa Maria del Fiore was finally completed between 1421 and 1436 by Brunelleschi, who added a dome that spanned nearly 138 feet at the base. This major Renaissance achievement is the Florentines' pride and joy. In speaking of his own project to build the dome of St. Peter's Basilica in Rome, Michelangelo will say: "I am going to build her sister, and though she will certainly be larger, she will in no way be more beautiful."

DAVID BY ANDREA DEL VERROCCHIO
Commissioned by the Medici, Andrea del Verrocchio's statue of David was sold to the city around 1476 and displayed in the Palazzo Vecchio, the government offices. Verrocchio is not only a sculptor but a goldsmith and painter, and this elegant work reflects the poetic climate then in full swing in Florence, which Michelangelo absorbs at the refined court of the Medici.

ST. GEORGE BY DONATELLO CHURCH OF ORSANMICHELE
The Church of Orsanmichele was destroyed in 1240, and a market took its place. In 1347 a new church was consecrated, and for this event each guild commissioned an artist to create a statue of its patron saint. For the armorer's guild, Donatello completed a marble statue of St. George in 1416. The future sculptor Michelangelo is particularly impressed by the natural confidence in St. George's pose and by the way Donatello gave life, spirit, and a sense of movement to a block of inanimate marble.

DEPOSITION BY FRA ANGELICO
The Deposition was painted around 1443 for the Strozzi Chapel of the Church of Santa Trinità by the Dominican friar Giovanni da Fiesole, better known as Fra Angelico. Thirty-five years after his death in 1455, Fra Angelico is famous throughout Italy for a style remarkable for its purity of line and its sparkling color, at times illuminated in gold. His art is representative of the supremacy of fifteenth-century Florentine painting.

11

Brunelleschi, portico of the Foundling Hospital, 1419-24, Florence

Masaccio, The Trinity, 1427,
Church of Santa Maria Novella, Florence

BRUNELLESCHI + DONATELLO
= THE ARRIVAL OF

At the beginning of the fifteenth century, a small group of artists sought to breathe new life into contemporary art. They began looking at the ancient sites of Rome in a whole new way, and in so doing they put the beauty of the classical works back at the center of artistic creativity. This period, known as the Quattrocento (meaning the 1400s), was the first phase of the Italian Renaissance.

Brunelleschi developed a new set of rules for architecture based on the combination of simple modular units. Donatello revived the tradition of working in bronze to express the power of the human form. In the area of paint-

Donatello, David, *1440-43, Bargello Museum, Florence*

Uccello, The Battle of San Romano, *1456, Uffizi Gallery, Florence*

+ MASACCIO + UCCELLO
THE RENAISSANCE

ing, Masaccio created a tragic and monumental vision of humanity that clearly broke with the medieval ideals. A short time later, Paolo Uccello explored the laws of mathematics, geometry, and perspective in an effort to create a more realistic form of artistic representation. All of these artists were trying to show humans at the center of the universe and to organize the world around humanity by means of rules that could be understood and applied to all forms of art. This ideal lies at the heart of Renaissance thinking, which reached its highest point in the Italy of the sixteenth century.

the master   assistant specialized in
painting figures   assistant specialized in
painting landscapes   assistant specialized in
painting architecture

14

GARZONI IS NOT
A PASTA DISH

In 1488, Michelangelo, thirteen years old, becomes an apprentice in the workshop of the famous Florentine painter Domenico Ghirlandaio. The workshops in big cities are efficiently organized to handle many orders at once. A hierarchy exists between the master, his apprentices, and their helpers, or *garzoni*.

Ghirlandaio specializes in frescoes. (*Fresco* is Italian for "fresh." The favorite Italian Renaissance technique of mural painting, it involves applying paint to a wall while the plaster is still wet, or "fresh." The completion of a fresco is a complex group effort.) Since 1486 he has been working on a commission from the banker Giovanni Tornabuoni for a series of frescoes depicting the lives of Mary and St. John the Baptist in the choir of the Church of Santa Maria Novella.

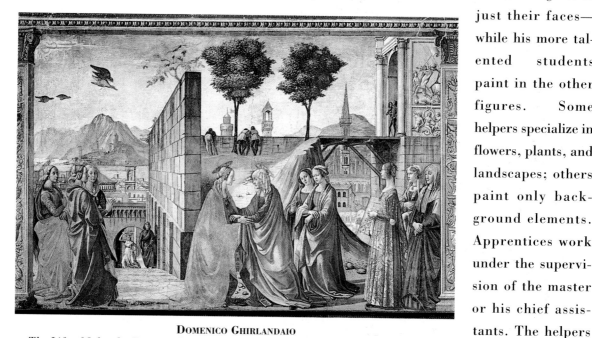

DOMENICO GHIRLANDAIO
The Life of John the Baptist: the Visitation (detail), 1486-90, choir of the Church of Santa Maria Novella, Florence.

Ghirlandaio himself has done the drawings, which his pupils will transfer to the walls. Then he will paint the most important parts of the fresco—the main figures or just their faces—while his more talented students paint in the other figures. Some helpers specialize in flowers, plants, and landscapes; others paint only background elements. Apprentices work under the supervision of the master or his chief assistants. The helpers grind the colors and prepare the plaster.

By putting many *garzoni* on a job, Ghirlandaio is able to expedite his orders and give his pupils the earliest opportunity of developing their practical skills. It is likely that Michelangelo was put to work on the Tornabuoni frescoes as soon as he arrived in Ghirlandaio's workshop.

After a year in Ghirlandaio's workshop, Michelangelo begins spending time in the Medici garden, a kind of academy where artists come together to study and copy the wonderful collection of art that this illustrious family has assembled. The curator of the collection is an aging pupil of Donatello's, the sculptor Bertoldo di Giovanni, and artists come to the garden to study under his supervision. Impressed by the young, talented Michelangelo, Lorenzo de' Medici takes him into his household and brings him up with his own sons. Growing up as part of this privileged and educated group, Michelangelo is constantly mingling with the intellectual elite of Florence. In fact, it is here that Michelangelo enhances his knowledge of literature and philosophy and begins to reflect on the ideals of love and harmony. The lavish court of the Medici had its origin in the fifteenth century, thanks to the financial success of the merchant-banker Cosimo de' Medici. A patron of the arts, he sponsored the work of artists, had the Medici palace and the Villa Careggi built, and financed the construction and decoration of religious buildings. His manuscript collection will form the basis of the Laurentian Library. Without officially holding public office, Cosimo and the Medici family control much of Florentine life. In thirty-eight years, Cosimo spends 663,775 florins (each one weighing 3.5 grams of gold) on buildings, charities, and taxes. Other wealthy Florentine families live on a scale similar to the Medici and equally contribute to the prestige of their city. Cosimo's grandson Lorenzo continues the family tradition of patronage to such a degree that he comes to be called Lorenzo the Magnificent. He adds to the existing collection of manuscripts and has a particular passion for medals, cameos, and precious stones. He has the Villa Poggio built in the town of Caiano and even owns a giraffe, which dies as a result of hitting its head on a low-hanging architectural detail. Respected and loved by his fellow Florentines, the statesman-poet Lorenzo dies in 1492.

"Some people think that this money would be better off in our coffers.
As for me, I believe that these expenditures are a credit to our house,
and that this capital has been put to good use." Lorenzo the Magnificent

MAGNIFICENT FOR ARTISTS

**HANDLED CUP WITH COVER
SARDONYX WITH SILVER GILT
MOUNTING**
*(Silver Museum, Florence)
The cup probably dates to the
fourth century, the mounting to the
sixteenth.*

GIULIANO DA SANGALLO
*Villa Poggio (Caiano)
Lorenzo bought this estate from the Strozzi family
and had it renovated between 1480 and 1485.*

JACOPO DA PONTORMO
*Portrait of Cosimo de' Medici,
1518-20 (Uffizi Gallery, Florence)
This is a retrospective portrait of
the man who was so beloved by the
Florentines that he was called "the
father of his country."*

MICHELOZZO DI BARTOLOMEO
*Library of the Convent of San
Marco, 1435-40 (Florence)
Cosimo had the convent entirely
rebuilt and financed the cost of the
furnishings, library, and
enlargement of the church.*

FRA ANGELICO
*Annunciation, 1440-41
(Convent of San Marco, Florence)
Cosimo commissioned Fra Angelico to paint frescoes on
the walls of the private cells of the monastery.*

DONATELLO
*Judith and Holofernes, 1456-57
(Palazzo Vecchio, Florence)
Commissioned in 1455 by Cosimo, this
dramatic bronze group was installed
in the Piazza della Signoria in 1595
as a symbol of the republic.*

BENOZZO GOZZOLI
*Journey of the Magi, 1459
(Palazzo Medici-Riccardi, Florence)
Lorenzo the Magnificent is
represented on horseback as the
youngest of the three Magi in this
masterpiece, which covers three
walls of a Medici chapel.*

SANDRO BOTTICELLI
*The Birth of Venus, 1486 (Uffizi Gallery, Florence)
This work was commissioned from Botticelli by Lorenzo
Pierofrancesco de' Medici, a cousin of Lorenzo the
Magnificent.*

FARNESE CUP, CAMEO IN AGATE
*(National Museum, Naples)
The cameo is antique. Lorenzo
bought the cup during a trip to
Rome.*

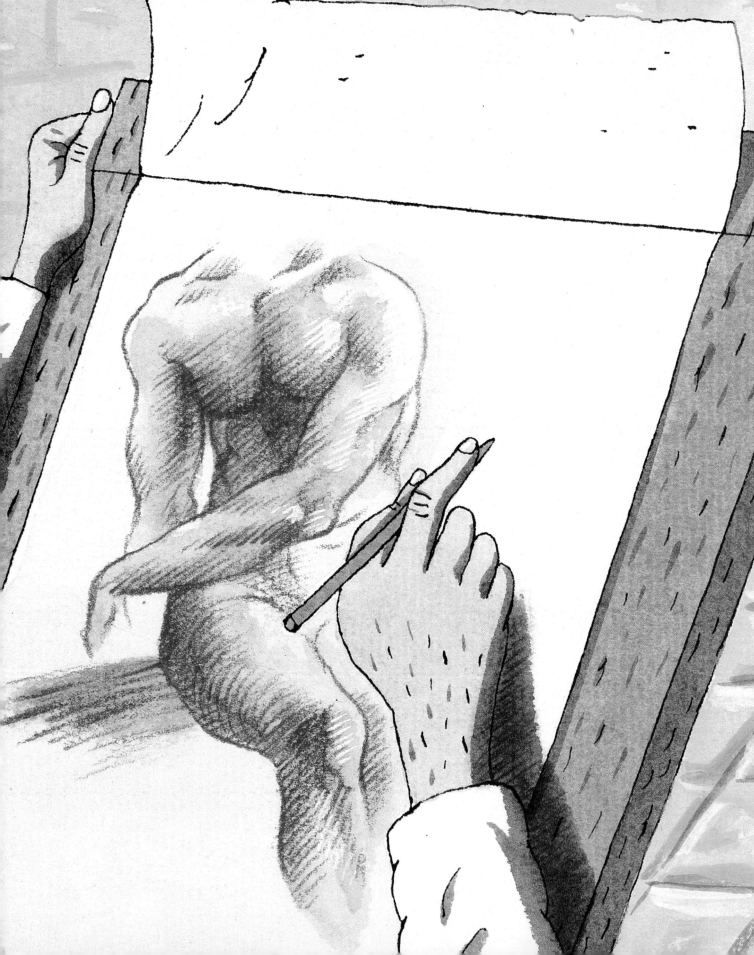

LOOK LIFELIKE,
STUDY THE DEAD

When Lorenzo de' Medici dies in 1492, Michelangelo goes back to his father's house. He is determined at this time to master the study of human anatomy by dissecting corpses.

The hospital in the monastery of Santo Spirito is one of the most important in Florence, and Michelangelo obtains permission (apparently from the hospital's chief administrator) to sketch in the morgue and dissect corpses. Dissection is not forbidden by the church, but obtaining corpses by digging them up certainly is.

Michelangelo's nude figures reveal a certain "life force" that can be directly traced to his intimate knowledge of the muscles of the body—knowledge he gains by studying the dead.

IF THEY STOOD UP,
HE'D BE FIVE FEET EIGHT
INCHES TALL,
SHE'D BE SEVEN FEET ONE

Pietà, *1499* ▶
St. Peter's Basilica,
Rome

In 1498, the French cardinal Jean de Bilhères de Lagraulas commissions Michelangelo to sculpt a statue to adorn his tomb. Michelangelo makes a *pietà* (from the Italian meaning "pity"), a representation of the Virgin holding the body of Christ across her knees following the descent from the cross. Christ's body follows the drapery of the Virgin's clothes. Her pose suggests a certain frailty and delicacy that adds to the religious mood of the piece.

In order for the body of Christ to fit harmoniously into the pyramidlike structure of the sculpture, Michelangelo treats the proportions in a most unusual way. The arms, legs, and hands of the Virgin are exaggerated, and it has been calculated that, if she were to stand up, she would be more than seven feet tall. This disproportion is masked by the abundant folds of her dress. On the other hand, her face is not in proportion to the rest of her body, being of the same dimensions as the face of Christ. Yet none of these unusual elements appears odd at first glance.

Mary is depicted as very young, and her face expresses beauty as an indication of a noble soul. To those who criticize him for making the Virgin too young to be Christ's mother, Michelangelo replies that her purity and virginity were proof against the effects of aging.

Michelangelo takes great care over the finish of the sculpture, polishing the marble with infinite patience to obtain an exceptional sheen.

The sculpture was placed in St. Peter's Basilica, and Vasari tells us that one day Michelangelo "went along to where the statue was and found a crowd of strangers from Lombardy singing its praises; then one of them asked another who had made it, only to be told: 'Our hunchback from Milan' [the nickname of another artist, Cristoforo Solari]. Michelangelo stood there not saying a word, but thinking it very odd to have all his efforts attributed to someone else. Then one night, taking his chisels, he shut himself in with a light and carved his name on the statue." He put his name on the sash over Mary's chest; it is the only work he will sign. The *Pietà* confirms Michelangelo's fame—and he is just twenty-four years old.

ARMS OF STEEL: THE MODERN,

The value attached to the art of the classical world is obvious in the rich collections that patrons assemble to enhance their prestige. The Romans of the Renaissance prize art objects from antiquity not only for their beauty but also for their value as examples of a glorious national heritage. Renaissance popes look on their collections as a sign of their political power.

In 1480 a statue of Apollo is discovered in the vineyards of Cardinal della Rovere and arouses universal acclaim; exhibited in the villa of the Belvedere in the Vatican, it soon becomes famous.

Upon his election as pope in 1503, Julius II asks the architect Bramante to build a courtyard in the Belvedere to display the Church's collection of classical sculptures, thereby founding the Vatican's collection of antiquities.

In January 1506 Michelangelo and Giuliano da Sangallo are on hand as one of the most renowned sculptures of the classical world is unearthed (again in a vineyard!). Through the writings of Pliny, scholars are able to identify the work as representing the divine retribution meted out to the Trojan priest Laocoön and his sons. Julius II buys the sculpture, and excavations in Rome multiply as people hope to make similar discoveries.

Apollo Belvedere
*Roman copy of a Greek original from the fourth century B.C.
Vatican Museum, Rome*

MICHELANGELO, TRIUMPHS

These statues are captivating by virtue of the beauty of their composition and the perfection with which they had been executed. Through his association with the Medici, Michelangelo has the opportunity to admire and study these models from antiquity; he even

tries to imitate them by sculpting a sleeping Cupid (1495), which he ages artificially by burying it (in a vineyard, of course). He later sells it as an original to a Roman collector. The collector discovers the hoax soon enough and seeks out its perpetrator, but far from being angry with Michelangelo, he forgives him and offers him a place to stay—meals included. In 1496 Michelangelo makes his first visit to Rome and has the opportunity to study new models from the classical world, in whose unsurpassed beauty he sees the ultimate challenge, a challenge that he meets by sculpting a *Bacchus*, the subject matter and style of which are inspired by Greek and Roman models.

But it is a few years later, back in Florence, that Michelangelo finally reveals his true genius and wins the battle of the Ancients and Moderns. He does this with *David*. Vasari writes of this masterpiece, "Without any doubt this figure has put in the shade every other statue, ancient or modern, Greek or Roman. . . . Anyone who has seen Michelangelo's *David* has no need to see anything else by any other sculptor, living or dead."

Michelangelo, David, *1501-4*
Academy of Fine Arts, Florence

VENICE

Venice, 1494 (19 years old): When the Medici, his patrons and protectors, fall out of favor and are temporarily expelled from Florence, Michelangelo flees to Venice, where he spends a short period.

BOLOGNA

Bologna, 1494 (19 years old): Michelangelo is taken under the wing of the learned Giovanfrancesco Aldovrandi, admirer of Florentine culture and literature. Michelangelo stays in his house for a year. He is commissioned to carve two marble statuettes for the shrine of St. Dominic.

Florence

Florence, 1495 (20 years old): The republic of Florence is under the virtual dictatorship of the Dominican Savonarola. Michelangelo returns to the city. He carves a sleeping Cupid, which is sold in Rome as an antique.

MICHELANGELO

Rome, 1496 (21 years old): Michelangelo carves the Bacchus for the banker and antiques collector Jacopo Galli. He is then commissioned to make a Pietà for a tomb in St. Peter's Basilica. He goes to Carrara to acquire the necessary marble.

CARRARA

Rome, 1505 (30 years old): Pope Julius II calls Michelangelo to Rome to work on his tomb. Michelangelo again spends time in Carrara choosing and preparing the marble.

Florence, 1506 (31 years old): Michelangelo returns to Florence in a fury after the pope refuses to receive him and pay for the marble he has chosen for the tomb.

Florence, 1501 (26 years old): Now famous, Michelangelo receives many commissions; the republic of Florence commissions him to carve the giant David.

Rome, 1506 (31 years old): Michelangelo resumes work on projects he had abandoned the year before. He refuses to return to Rome despite requests from the pope.

Florence, 1517 (42 years old): Pope Leo X commissions Michelangelo to make the facade of the Church of San Lorenzo in Florence. Other commissions, such as the Medici sacristy and tombs, keep him in the city.

FERRARA

Florence, 1508 (33 years old): Michelangelo returns to the city for a few weeks to settle his affairs before leaving for Rome.

Ferrara, 1529 (54 years old): Political events require Michelangelo to study military architecture. He visits Ferrara to look over that city's fortifications.

ON THE MOVE

Florence, 1534 (59 years old): Michelangelo returns to Florence to resume work on the Medici Library, which he began ten years earlier.

BOLOGNA

Rome, 1532 (57 years old): Michelangelo signs a fifth contract with the heirs of Julius II for his tomb. Pope Clement VII asks Michelangelo for new decorations for the altar wall of the Sistine Chapel.

Bologna, 1507 (32 years old): Michelangelo meets Julius II for a reconciliation. The pope commissions an overlife-size memorial statue of himself to be cast in bronze. It takes Michelangelo a year to complete the statue (it is pulled down and destroyed in 1511).

Rome, 1508 (33 years old): Michelangelo begins work on the ceiling of the Sistine Chapel (1508-12). Pope Julius II dies in 1513, and Michelangelo resumes work on Julius's tomb, carving Moses and the Slaves (1513-16).

Rome

Rome, 1534 (59 years old): Michelangelo begins work on the Last Judgment (1536-41). In 1535 Pope Paul III appoints Michelangelo his chief painter, sculptor, and architect. Michelangelo increases the number of architectural projects in Rome. Despite pleas from his fellow Florentines and Grand Duke Cosimo de' Medici, Michelangelo never returns to Florence, considering himself too old to make the trip once again.

25

IF A CUBIC METER OF MARBLE WEIGHS OVER TWO TONS, HOW HEAVY IS DAVID?

Michelangelo prefers marble to all other materials because it is a stone of enormous value, prized for its whiteness and sheen. Cutting marble is difficult because it is both hard and extremely fragile.

The most beautiful Italian marble comes from the mountains of Carrara. In Michelangelo's time, the marble is extracted by drilling holes into the rock, inserting wooden wedges into the holes, and then soaking the wedges with water, so that as they expand the stone breaks away. The blocks are then slid down the mountains with ropes and transported to the nearest road on rollers. There they are put on carts to be taken to the closest port. The preferred means of transport is by sea or river, since these are both quicker and less likely to damage the cargo with bumping.

On various occasions Michelangelo spends periods of several months in Carrara, selecting the quality, shape, and size of the blocks with great care and supervising the quarrying and even the transportation of the marble.

When the blocks of marble for Pope Julius II's tomb arrive in Rome, they take up fully half of St. Peter's Square, to the amazement of the general public.

To sculpt his *David* (1501-4), Michelangelo uses a block of marble in which, according to Vasari, "Simone da Fiesole had started to carve a giant figure and had bungled the work so badly that he had hacked a hole between the legs and left the block completely botched and misshapen." Even so, "Michelangelo worked a miracle in restoring to life something that had been left for dead."

When Michelangelo finished the statue, its great size (it's over thirteen feet high and weighs more than five metric tons—more than 11,000 pounds!) "provoked endless disputes over the best way to transport it . . . Giuliano da Sangallo, with his brother Antonio, constructed a very strong wooden framework and suspended the statue from it with ropes so that when moved it would sway gently without being broken; then they drew it along by means of winches over planks laid on the ground and put it in place."

HOW ABOUT LIKE THIS?

Michelangelo sculpted his impressive figure of David between 1501 and 1504. This represented a real feat of technical prowess, and the fact that he was sculpting a block that another sculptor had already worked forty years before only made his task all the more difficult. From the day it was first revealed to the public to today, *David* has inspired comments from scholars, such as Charles de Tolnay:

"**T**he concept of strength as a virtue completely determines the attitude of Michelangelo's David and explains its tense expression. The whole weight of the figure falls on the right leg and the body sways slightly toward this side.... Thus there exists a contrast between the two sides of the statue.... This contrast of sides corresponds to a moral distinction.... The Middle Ages gave a theological interpretation to this distinction, namely, that the strong right side is under divine protection, the weak left exposed to the powers of evil."

"**T**he body of the David was something entirely new for Michelangelo himself. His early concern for rhythmic forces within the body is here replaced by an exact rendition of human anatomy; the richness of forms in bones, muscles, veins, and soft parts in the breast and belly is extraordinary. The finest surface gradations are given; there is an all-pervasive tension as though the body were a veritable reservoir of energies. Every organ of the human body in nature suggests its function by its form even without movement. Michelangelo recognized this principle. By making intensively visible the essential structure of organs at rest, he is able to suggest potential action."

"**I**t would seem that Michelangelo is seeking to express not a particular transitory moment in David's life, but rather the hero's unchanging character and moral attitude toward life. He is the incarnation of fearless moral strength.... The marble David of Michelangelo may be regarded as a sort of synthesis of the ideals of the Florentine Renaissance. In the accurate anatomy one finds the vigorous forms and the proud visage is recognizable the heroic conception of man as a free creature and as master of Fate."

"**T**he sculptor has suppressed all the usual attributes except the slingshot, and even this is hidden behind the back of the figure. There exist several theories as to how David could make immediate use of the slingshot. These are based on the supposition that the statue represents the moment before the flinging of the stone. However, the figure actually holds the stone in the right hand, and the end of the slingshot in the left; consequently, the slingshot cannot be used immediately. It is necessary to deduce that Michelangelo did not wish to represent a definite moment in the life of David. He wished to incarnate in this figure the essence of his character, strength, and courage. To express this idea, Michelangelo has associated his David with the Hercules type."

"**T**hus Michelangelo's David embodies the qualities of a true patriot: he is a citizen prepared for war. Michelangelo identified David with Hercules in order to better show his virtues. It is not surprising that Michelangelo combined the two concepts in a sculpture that was intended to stir local pride: Hercules had been honored as the patron and protector of Florence since the thirteenth century and was depicted on the city's seal. Vasari understood this perfectly: 'This was intended as a symbol of liberty for the Palace, signifying that just as David had protected his people and governed them justly, so whoever ruled Florence should vigorously defend the city and govern it with justice.'"

THE LAOCOÖN
circa 150 B.C.
Discovered in 1506, this sculptural group gains international fame (in 1515 King Francis I of France almost succeeds in carting it off as war booty). Excavations mushroom, attracting collectors and ambassadors from various European courts, all of them eager to acquire antique masterpieces.

THE FORUM
The modernization of Rome turns the city into one huge construction site; in so doing, some remarkable classical remains are unearthed. All that digging, however, often destroys more than it preserves, despite warnings from scholars. By the end of the fifteenth century, the Forum has been turned into a quarry. Pope Paul III finally closes it in 1540, permitting access only to those building the new St. Peter's Basilica.

BUSINESS IS

CAPITOL SQUARE
In 1530 Pope Paul III launches a program of renovation and development of one of the most important parts of ancient Rome, the Capitol. Michelangelo wins the commission and prepares new designs—but the work is not completed until 110 years later.

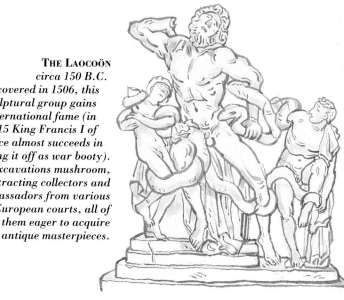

BRAMANTE'S TEMPIETTO
This temple is built between 1502 and 1510 at Saint Peter in Montorio, the supposed site of the saint's martyrdom, by Donato Bramante. The temple is round with ancient-style columns, clear allusions to classical buildings.

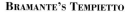

THE TRIUMPH OF GALATEA, VILLA FARNESINA, BY RAPHAEL
After his successes in the Vatican, Raphael is much sought after by private patrons and comes to dominate the painting community in Rome. He paints this fresco for the ornate walkway of the Villa Farnesina, built by Baldassare Peruzzi for a banker named Chigi.

Rome is the center of extraordinary artistic activity during the fifteenth and sixteenth centuries. The sack of the city by the troops of Charles V in 1527 checks this rise only momentarily. The political ambitions of the popes leads to many public works being undertaken to embellish the city: certain areas are reconstructed, palaces are built, civil and religious buildings are given painted and sculpted decorations. In all this, the artists and their patrons blend their love of classical antiquities, their passion for collecting, and their desire to modernize the city.

BOOMING

THE SCHOOL OF ATHENS, VATICAN, BY RAPHAEL
The bustle of creativity in Rome and the rediscovery of ancient works attract many artists to the city, leading to much competition. Raphael arrives from Urbino and decorates the pope's apartments (including this painting of ancient Greek philosophers) while Michelangelo is busy working on the nearby Sistine Chapel. Michelangelo doesn't like Raphael and accuses him of stealing his ideas.

THE FARNESE PALACE
Built of blocks plundered from ancient buildings, this is the largest private palace in Rome. It's named for the Farnese family, one of whose members becomes pope as Paul III. It is begun by Antonio da Sangallo the Younger, but on his death Michelangelo takes over as chief architect.

A TASTE FOR THE GROTESQUE
Digging around under Trajan's baths, workers find remains of Nero's palace (Rome is full of this stuff). These underground rooms, or grottoes, are decorated with paintings of fantastic scenes in a style that comes to be known as grotesque. It has a considerable influence on contemporary artists.

CASTEL SANT'ANGELO
Originally built as Hadrian's mausoleum, this massive construction is decorated and fortified as a place of refuge for the popes during times of danger (it's connected to the Vatican by a secret passage).

Construction of the Sistine Chapel begins in 1473, and it is decorated by the leading painters of the fifteenth century. The ceiling is simply a blue sky scattered with gold and silver stars to evoke the celestial vault.

The fresco technique consists of painting on fresh, damp, lime plaster. As the plaster dries, it incorporates the paint in the material of the wall, making for a very hard and lasting surface. The painting must be done quickly, and only a small section at a time.

Michelangelo is commissioned to paint the twelve apostles, but after a few preliminary sketches he is not satisfied with the result. With the pope's approval, he decides to change the theme.

In 1508, Michelangelo asks colleagues from Florence to come to Rome to assist him, since they are more experienced in fresco work. They work under his supervision, providing minor scenes and the decorative parts of the work.

When mold appears on the first frescoes to be painted, Michelangelo is discouraged and wants abandon the project. Then it is discovered that t much water was used in the plaster mixture. Usi less water, Michelangelo goes back to work.

By 1510, half of the ceiling has been completed, but then the pope's financing stops, and so does the work. Michelangelo is able to resume his efforts in 1511.

Michelangelo permits no one to see the work in progress except the impatient Julius II. In a fit of rage, the pope insists on having the ceiling uncovered even though it is still incomplete.

The chapel ceiling is finally officially opened on October 3 1512. Michelangelo, who wanted so much to be recognize for his gifts as a sculptor, will now become world famous as a painter.

"I'M A SCULPTOR, NOT A PAINTER!"

In 1505 Pope Julius II summons Michelangelo to Rome to carve his tomb. A great patron of the arts, the pope wants this project to be carried out during his lifetime. Michelangelo plans a vast monument designed to be placed inside St. Peter's Basilica.

To accommodate Michelangelo's plans, Julius II arranges to have the basilica rebuilt and challenges his favorite architect, Giuliano da Sangallo, and the talented and ambitious Donato Bramante to compete for the project. Bramante's design wins the pope's endorsement, and a despairing Sangallo sees his prestige at the papal court diminish.

Faced with a project as enormous as the basilica, the pope loses interest in the construction of his tomb. Convinced that Bramante has had something to do with the pope's change of mind, Michelangelo becomes discouraged and returns to Florence. Michelangelo is right. As Vasari tells it, "Bramante was constantly plotting with Raphael to remove from the pope's mind the idea of having Michelangelo finish the tomb.... He and Raphael suggested to Pope

Julius that if the tomb were finished it would bring nearer the day of his death, and they said that it was bad luck to have one's tomb built while one was still alive. Eventually they persuaded his holiness to get Michelangelo on his return to paint...the ceiling of the chapel in the Vatican. In this way Bramante and Michelangelo's other rivals thought they would divert his energies from sculpture, in which they realized he was supreme. This, they argued, would make things hopeless for him, since as he had no experience of coloring in fresco he would certainly...do less creditable work as a painter. ...So when Michelangelo returned to Rome he found the pope resolved to leave the tomb as it was for the time being, and he was told to paint the ceiling of the chapel. Michelangelo...tried in every possible way to shake the burden off his shoulders. But the more he refused, the more determined he made the pope, who was a willful man by nature.... Seeing that his holiness was persevering, Michelangelo resigned himself to doing what he was asked."

NOTHING LESS THAN A MASTERPIECE

The Sistine Chapel is built according to the proportions of Solomon's Temple, as described in the Book of Kings: the length, 132 feet, is approximately twice the height, about 67 feet, and three times the width of 44 feet. To help with the enormous task, Michelangelo calls on several Florentine painters, including Francesco Granacci, his old friend from his apprenticeship days in Ghirlandaio's workshop. But the work takes such a long time that one by one his colleagues grow tired of it and depart. Alone with his helpers, who prepare the plaster surface and the paint, Michelangelo finishes the second half of the ceiling in twenty months.

The Sistine Chapel ceiling tells the story of the beginning of man as told in the Bible, from the creation of Adam to the coming of Moses. Michelangelo creates imaginary architecture to contain the various scenes, including painted thrones, arches, and columns.

His contemporaries are awestruck by the vivid colors and especially by the sheer beauty and power of the 340 figures that fill the curved surface of the chapel ceiling.

Here is Michelangelo in scale with the Sistine Chapel ceiling he decorated. It doesn't seem so surprising that he took four years to finish his masterpiece.

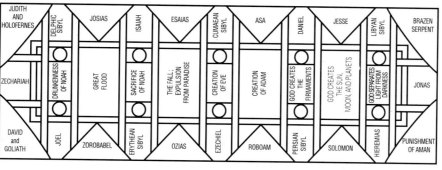

JUDITH AND HOLOFERNES	DELPHIC SIBYL	JOSIAS	ISAIAH	ESAIAS	CUMAEAN SIBYL	ASA	DANIEL	JESSE	LIBYAN SIBYL	BRAZEN SERPENT
ZECHARIAH	DRUNKENNESS OF NOAH	GREAT FLOOD	SACRIFICE OF NOAH	THE FALL; EXPULSION FROM PARADISE	CREATION OF EVE	CREATION OF ADAM	GOD CREATES THE FIRMAMENTS	GOD CREATES THE SUN, MOON, AND PLANETS	GOD SEPARATES LIGHT FROM DARKNESS	JONAS
DAVID and GOLIATH	JOEL	ZOROBABEL	ERYTHEAN SIBYL	OZIAS	EZECHIEL	ROBOAM	PERSIAN SIBYL	SOLOMON	HIEREMIAS	PUNISHMENT OF AMAN

35

COMING DOWN FROM THE CEILING, MICHELANGELO FINDS HIMSELF IN THE MIDST OF VERY EARTHLY PROBLEMS

I've grown a goiter dwelling in this den—
the way cats do from streams in Lombardy
unless that's in some other land—
but it pushes my belly close under my chin.

With my beard turned up to heaven, may nape
fallen in atop my hump;
I'm growing a harpy's breast;
and the brush-drops fall to bedew my face
and create there a rich embroidery.

My loins grind into my belly,
my buttock like a crupper bears my weight;
my unguided feet wander aimlessly.

In front my skin becomes loose and stretched
behind it grows more taught and wrinkled,
and I bend like a Syrian bow.

So the reasoning that my mind creates
comes out false and quaint, I know,
for poorly aims a gun with barrel bent.

So come then, Giovanni, and try
to defend my dead pictures and my fame,
since I fare poorly and my painting is my shame

MICHELANGELO

The four years of hard work on the Sistine Chapel ceiling leave Michelangelo exhausted. His contemporary Giorgio Vasari writes that Michelangelo "executed the frescoes in great discomfort, having to work with his face looking upwards, which impaired his sight so badly that he could not read or look at drawings save with his head turned backwards; and this lasted for several months afterwards." Michelangelo complains of all his afflictions in the poem above, written to his close friend Giovanni da Pistoia.

When Michelangelo climbs down off his scaffolding, he finds himself once again immersed in the preoccupations of daily life. Payments from the pope are erratic. "Here it is thirteen months now and I haven't see a cent from the pope," he writes in 1508. The situation leaves him in financial straits.

Michelangelo hires someone to take care of his household, but when that person expresses an interest in learning how to draw from the master and becomes less diligent in his duties, the artist blows up: "Here I find myself with this stinking idiot who says he doesn't want to lose time, that he wants to learn...I need someone to help me, and if this person doesn't think he can fit the bill, then I needn't shell out another penny on him."

Amid all his troubles, though, Michelangelo feels the overwhelming weight of fatigue and solitude. He writes to his father: "I live here in great toil and great weariness of body. I have no friends of any kind and don't want any. I don't even have time to eat."

When his older brother Leonardo becomes a Dominican friar, Michelangelo finds himself in the role of the eldest son with new responsibilities for his father, Lodovico, who does not work, his brothers Buonarroto and Giovan Simone, for whom he buys a business, and Gismondo, whom he sets up with property near Florence. In 1512, he writes: "In all these nearly fourteen years I have not had an hour of peace; everything I have done was with the purpose of coming to your aid, and you have never recognized or believed that. May God forgive you all. I am ready to do the same again for as long as I am alive and have the energy to do so."

APOLLONIUS OF ATHENS
BELVEDERE TORSO

Circa 50 B.C. This classical statue, exhibited in the Belvedere in the Vatican since the beginning of the sixteenth century, owes its fame in part to Michelangelo's admiration of it, despite its fragmentary condition. He said of it, "It is the work of a man who knew the human form better than nature itself."

MICHELANGELO'S "UNFINISHED" STYLE

Michelangelo's sculptures have always posed a particular problem: he left many of them unfinished. His early works had already assured his reputation: the *Bacchus* of 1497 (Florence, Bargello Museum), the *Pietà* of 1499 (Rome, St. Peter's Basilica), and the *David* of 1504 (Florence, Academy of Fine Arts) are perfectly finished, but such is not the case for later works. Of course, a defect in the marble, a heavy workload, or the need to visit another town are all good excuses to abandon a sculpture halfway, but this does not explain everything. Fully aware of Michelangelo's genius, both friends and patrons were content to accept unfinished works and appreciated them as they stood.

PITTI TONDO

1504-5 (Bargello Museum, Florence)
Michelangelo makes this circular relief, or tondo, for the patron Bartolommeo Pitti. Called to Rome by Pope Julius II in 1505, he delivers it unfinished. Pitti accepts the piece, even though it was incomplete.

RONDANINI PIETÀ

1555-64 (Castello Sforzesco, Milan)
Michelangelo works on this sculpture for ten years, continually changing its composition and working on three different versions in the same block of stone. The arm of Christ, which does not fit with the final design, seems to be a holdover from some earlier version. In all probability, Michelangelo would have removed it, but his death intervened.

SLAVE, CALLED THE DYING SLAVE

1513-16 (Musée du Louvre, Paris)
Michelangelo begins sculpting this slave, which was intended for the tomb of Julius II, in 1513. The legs, torso, and left arm are polished and finished. At the base, however, there is not enough marble to carve the left foot and maintain the stability of the statue. This is probably why the piece remains unfinished.

THE SLAVE ATLAS
1532-34 (Academy of Fine Arts, Florence)
This sculpture is one of a series of five intended for Julius II's tomb, although they are not included in the final plans. Despite the fact that they are unfinished, they are still much admired. A sixteenth-century guide to Florence considered them to be superior to Michelangelo's finished works because they more clearly express his artistic ideas.

BRUTUS

Circa 1540 (Bargello Museum, Florence)
While working on the fresco of the Last Judgment, Michelangelo starts this bust of Brutus, Caesar's assassin, for some Florentine exiles who wish to commemorate a different assassination: that of Alessandro de' Medici by his cousin Lorenzo. Michelangelo gives it unfinished to Tiberio Calcagni in 1555, who then sculpts the drapery and part of the neck and chin.

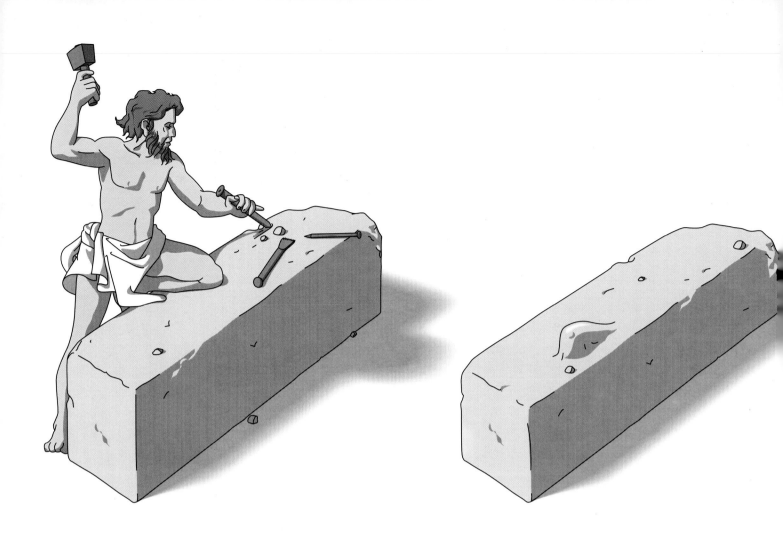

FREEING THE FIGURE FROM

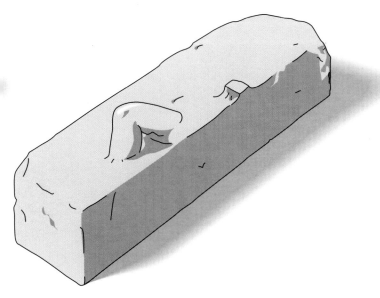

THE STONE

Despite the energy with which Michelangelo carves stone, his method is not merely to give rein to an irresistible urge to create, powered by the imagination alone. He makes sketches to work out a harmonious and balanced composition, then more complete drawings, and finally little wax or clay models that allow him to see what the piece will look like three dimensionally.

He then draws the figure on the block of stone and starts sculpting. Vasari describes the process: "One must take a figure of wax or some other firm material and lay it horizontally in a vessel of water; then, as the water is, of course, flat and level, when the figure is raised little by little above the surface the more salient parts are revealed first, while the lower parts . . . remain submerged, until eventually it all comes into view. In the same way figures must be carved out of marble by the chisel; the parts in the highest relief must be revealed first and then little by little the lower parts." Working this way, the figure appears to gradually free itself from the stone.

1- Hammer 2- Pointed chisels
3- Tooth-edged chisel 4- Chisels
5- Rasps

Michelangelo uses the standard tools of his trade: hammers and pointed chisels, which he uses to shape the block, and chisels with serrated edges that leave parallel striations, fine or coarse, depending on the tool. Michelangelo uses these as if he were drawing on paper, forming a network of sculpted lines that crisscross and allow volume to be suggested.

Michelangelo begins work on this marble figure of St. Matthew, nearly nine feet high, in 1506 to decorate the interior of Florence's Cathedral of Santa Maria del Fiore. The most prominent sections, the left knee and thigh, are almost finished, while the outer edges of the upper statue have been worked more superficially. He never finished this statue.

MICHELANGELO
CAN YOU RECOGNIZE HIM AMONG

During Michelangelo's life, Europe is dominated by powerful and glittering courts, such as those of Venice, Milan, and Madrid. Royal or princely reputation is measured in terms of status symbols, which include pomp, elegance, and the display of wealth, such as costly works of art. It's a good time to be a popular artist.

The pope rules one of the most important states in Italy, but he is also spiritual leader of the Christian world and thus involved in the affairs of all Western countries. Foreign dignitaries, both political and religious, flock to the papal court and form a cosmopolitan community. Like any king or prince, the pope seeks to demonstrate his power by living the lifestyle of the rich and famous.

IS IN ROME
THESE SIX CHARACTERS?

The papal court is a place of intrigues, where the ambitions of kings, cardinals, noble families, and even artists clash. Much money is spent on clothes, jewels, and sumptuous banquets. Which one of these six characters do you think is Michelangelo?

ANSWER: *No, V. Michelangelo works on commissions for seven popes, but his personal style does not reflect the sumptuous Vatican court. Condivi tells us,* "Michelangelo has always been very abstemious in his way of life, taking food more out of necessity than for pleasure, and especially while he has work in progress, when he most often contents himself with a piece of bread, which he eats while working. . . . I have often heard him say, 'Ascanio, however rich I may have been, I have always lived like a poor man.' And just as he has eaten sparingly, so also he has done with little sleep, since according to him, has seldom done him good, for when he sleeps he almost always suffers from headaches; in fact, too much sleep gives him a bad stomach. When he was more robust he often slept in his clothes and in his boots. . . . and he has sometimes gone so long without taking them off that then the skin came away like a snake's with the boots."

FIRST DESIGN: 1505

Pope Julius II is planning his future tomb. In order to fulfill his patron's ambitions, Michelangelo designs a grandiose structure that occupies an area of nearly 800 square feet. Large bronze reliefs and forty marble statues on three levels are to tell the story of the pope's life. Such a work could only be located in St. Peter's Basilica.

SECOND DESIGN: 1513

Work on the tomb is interrupted by the rebuilding of the basilica but then starts up again with the death of the pope in 1513. His relatives sign a new contract with Michelangelo. The general design is modified: the tomb will not be free-standing but will be fixed to the wall. Michelangelo works at it feverishly for three years, sculpting the two Slaves (in the Louvre) and the statue of Moses, incorporated in the final work.

THIRD DESIGN: 1516

Giovanni de' Medici is now pope (as Leo X) and commissions Michelangelo to work on the façade of Florence's Church of San Lorenzo. When Michelangelo stops work on the tomb to work on the church, he is harassed by Julius II's inheritors, so he presents a third plan in which the tomb is shorter and has a simpler, less decorated façade. Then Giulio de' Medici becomes pope (as Clement VII) and commissions Michelangelo to build the new sacristy of San Lorenzo. In 1525, Michelangelo proposes an even simpler fourth plan for the tomb, but Julius II's descendants reject it.

FIFTH DESIGN: 1532

Political events keep Michelangelo in Florence. Finally back in Rome, he negotiates a fifth contract for the tomb. This plan resembles the third but is further simplified, and the tomb is no longer to be placed in the St. Peter's Basilica, but in the Church of San Pietro in Vincoli. By then (1535), the pope is Paul III, who repeats Clement VII's commission for the fresco of the Last Judgment in the Sistine Chapel and demands that Michelangelo start work on it immediately.

TOMB OF JULIUS II
Church of San Pietro in Vincoli
In 1542, Michelangelo puts forward a sixth and final contract, invalidating all previous ones and entrusting several different sculptors with finishing the statues and decoration in order to complete the tomb. This is finally finished and installed in January 1545. On the upper level are the Virgin and Child, Julius II's effigy, the Prophet, the Sibyl; in the lower tier are Active Life, Moses and Contemplative Life, sculpted by Michelangelo. Moses is the only statue from the 1513 project to make it to the final 1545 version.

Condivi called it "the tragedy of the tomb," and Michelangelo agreed, writing near the end of his life, "I wasted all my youth chained to that tomb." When Julius II summoned him to Rome in 1505 to build the tomb, Michelangelo took on this important project without realizing that circumstances would conspire to delay its completion. He found himself forced to constantly battle with the relatives of Julius II on the one hand, who were indignant about his failure to fulfill signed contracts, and on the other with a series of popes who obliged him to work for them. He was able to devote time to Julius II's tomb only intermittently, which is why it took him forty years. Every time the contract was renegotiated, the project became more modest, with fewer statues: of the forty originally planned, only six were executed, only three of them by Michelangelo. The terrible Julius II haunted Michelangelo for thirty years after his death.

45

RICHELIEU INSTALLS THE STATUES IN HIS CHATEAU IN POITOU.

1749: RICHELIEU HAS THE "SLAVES" BROUGHT FROM HIS DISTANT CHATEAU IN THE PROVINCES TO HIS TOWNHOUSE IN PARIS, A LOCALE ALREADY FAMOUS FOR HIS AMOROUS INTRIGUES . . .

I HAVE FREED MY "SLAVES." NATURE WILL BE WITNESS TO THEIR SUFFERING.

DURING THE REVOLUTION THEY ARE SEIZED AS ÉMIGRÉ PROPERTY.

THEY ARE STORED AWAY BEFORE BEING PUBLICLY AUCTIONED.

I HOPE THAT THE MUSEUM OF FRENCH MONUMENTS IS ABLE TO FIND A HOME FOR THESE TWO VOYAGERS.

VERY WELL, MY DEAR CITIZEN LENOIR, THESE TWO SCULPTURES WILL BE EXCLUDED FROM THE COMING PUBLIC AUCTION.

TALK ABOUT BEING HEAVY!

LISTEN, OUR JOB'LL BE OVER IN NO TIME, THEIRS IS FOREVER.

OPEN SINCE 1793, THE CENTRAL MUSEUM OF THE ARTS IS LOCATED IN THE LOUVRE. SINCE THE MUSEUM DEMANDS THE MOST PRESTIGIOUS ARTWORK FOR ITS COLLECTIONS, IT IS ONLY NATURAL THAT MICHELANGELO'S "SLAVES" SHOULD CROSS ITS THRESHOLD ON AUGUST 28, 1794, TO BECOME ONE OF THE MUSEUM'S MOST GLORIOUS TREASURES.

COMING UP

Pope Clement VII is eager to have Michelangelo paint the altar wall of the Sistine Chapel, but he dies in 1534. His successor, Paul III, renews the project and demands that Michelangelo carry out the fresco of the *Last Judgment*.

Michelangelo wants to use all of the wall; to do this he has two windows walled up and destroys the frescoes that had previously adorned the chapel, as well as a small part of his own work on the ceiling. The resulting surface is immense: 44 feet 6 inches high, 39 feet 7 inches wide.

The painter Sebastiano del Piombo is supposed to prepare the wall but uses a coating suitable only for oil paints. Furious, Michelangelo has this surface removed and reprepares the wall for a fresco, which delays the start of the work.

Michelangelo is finally able to begin painting in 1536. Paul III, the only person allowed to visit the work in progress, watches it develop with eager impatience. It is eventually unveiled in 1541, after six years of toil. The pope is overwhelmed and is said to fall to his knees, begging God to have mercy on him on Judgment Day.

The composition turns in a huge circular movement around the pivot of Christ as judge. On the left, the dead rise from their tombs and

are carried toward Christ by wingless angels. On the right, the damned descend into Hell and are pushed out of Charon's boat by blows from his oar. (In ancient mythology, Charon was the ferryman who transported the spirits of the dead.) The terrifying figure of Christ is flanked by the Virgin Mary and martyred saints, including, seated at the center of the painting, Saint Bartholomew holding his skin (he was flayed alive) on which Michelangelo has depicted his own distorted face.

Michelangelo revolutionized the traditional iconography of the Last Judgment; there are no fantastic demons or tortures of the damned.

OR GOING DOWN?

Michelangelo shows man realizing the consequences of his own actions, horribly aware of his own responsibility for his fall.

The painting met with general approval for its artistic value, but the nudity of the figures was criticized. While the work was still in progress, Pope Paul III's master of ceremonies complained, saying (according to Vasari) that "it was most disgraceful that in so sacred a place there should have been depicted all those nude figures, exposing themselves so shamefully, and that it was no work for a papal chapel but rather for the public baths and taverns." Michelangelo took his revenge by depicting this man as Minos, the judge in Hell.

Paul III, a fervent admirer of the artist, defended Michelangelo in spite of continuous criticism. A few years later, however, Pope Paul IV decided to cover up the more flagrant examples of nudity. Daniele da Volterra was hired to paint clothes on the nudes, thereby earning himself the nickname *Braghettone* ("breeches maker"). Later popes proved even more bashful; more clothing was painted on at the end of the sixteenth century and then even more in the seventeenth and eighteenth.

1

2

5

6

SHE IS HANDSOME

According to Vasari, Michelangelo refused to paint "anything save the human body in its most beautifully proportioned and perfect forms." Hence his dislike of doing portraits. Perfect physical beauty represented a philosophical ideal for him, one in which Beauty is the child of Reason. He painted faces of harmonious proportions with straight noses and full mouths, faces that displayed a soft melancholy.

Can you tell which of these faces are those of men, and which are of women?

4

8

HE IS PRETTY

HIS DEAR COLLEAGUES

Michelangelo always had a reputation for being a timid and solitary man, suspicious and moody by nature, who did not get along well with his fellow artists. Hence the romantic notion of Michelangelo as a misunderstood, unloved genius. What was the real story?

FOR

ASCANIO CONDIVI (1525-74), painter and writer
Assistant and disciple of Michelangelo, he is best known for his *Life of Michelangelo*, published in Rome in 1553. He undoubtedly wrote the book at Michelangelo's request in response to Vasari's 1550 work, which the artist did not consider entirely accurate.

FRANCESCO GRANACCI (1469-1574), painter
One of Michelangelo's childhood friends. While apprenticing in Ghirlandaio's workshop, he encouraged Michelangelo to do the same and later introduced him to the Medici garden, where Michelangelo learned how to sculpt. Despite a few rough periods in their relationship, they always remained close friends.

LEONE LEONI (1509-90) sculptor and medalist
Leoni struck a medal with an exceedingly fine portrait of the artist and offered it—two in silver and two in bronze—to Michelangelo as a token of his esteem. This gift pleased Michelangelo so much that in return he sent a wax model of his *Hercules and Antaeus*.

SEBASTIANO DEL PIOMBO (1485-1547), painter
Sebastiano met Michelangelo in Rome in 1511. They became close friends, and on various occasions Michelangelo provided him with sketches for his artistic projects.

GIULIANO DA SANGALLO (1445-1516), architect, military engineer, sculptor
It was probably due to his influence that Michelangelo was summoned to Rome in 1505 by Julius II to work on the pope's tomb. Giuliano also gave the artist advice when there were technical problems relating to the painting of the Sistine Chapel ceiling.

GIORGIO VASARI (1511-74), painter, architect, writer
In his biography of Michelangelo, Vasari professed a deep admiration for the artist and believed that the glory of Florentine art was embodied in his works. He was in charge of Michelangelo's funeral and the design for his tomb in the Church of Santa Croce in Florence.

DANIELE DA VOLTERRA (1509-66), painter and sculptor
One of Michelangelo's most fervent admirers, he was commissioned to paint loincloths and other clothing on the naked figures in Michelangelo's *Last Judgment*, earning the nickname *Braghettone* ("breeches maker").

AGAINST

BACCIO BANDINELLI (1493-1560), sculptor and painter
Michelangelo's imitator and Florentine rival, Bandinelli was jealous of the artist's talent. The two fought over the right to carve a huge block of marble into a counterpart to Michelangelo's *David* for the Piazza della Signoria in Florence.

DONATO BRAMANTE (1444-1514), architect
Bramante influenced Pope Julius II in promoting his talented relative Raphael over Giuliano da Sangallo and Michelangelo. Michelangelo accused him of dishonesty and maliciousness. It was Bramante who persuaded Julius II to abandon the construction of his tomb, thus depriving Michelangelo of a commission that would later prove to be difficult to complete.

LEONARDO DA VINCI (1452-1519), painter and architect
Leonardo was admired for this many talents, his good looks, intelligence, and sophistication. Was Michelangelo jealous of him? The hostility he felt toward Leonardo was legendary. The two men competed in the arts and on occasion exchanged caustic remarks. Leonardo once extolled the superiority of painting over sculpture, which he claimed was a messy art; this remark made Michelangelo extremely angry.

RAPHAEL SANTI (RAPHAEL SANZIO) (1483-1520), painter
Michelangelo resented Raphael, saying of him: "Everything he knows about art, he got from me." Legend has it that one day Michelangelo crossed paths with Raphael and said to him, "There you are, always escorted like a prince!" to which Raphael responded, "What about you? Alone and sad-faced like an executioner?"

ANTONIO DA SANGALLO THE YOUNGER (1485-1546), architect and military engineer
Michelangelo was highly critical of Sangallo's new model for St. Peter's Basilica. Sangallo and his followers, whom Vasari dubbed the "Sangallo clique," tried to stop Michelangelo from receiving architectural commissions. When Michelangelo took over the basilica project on Sangallo's death, Sangallo's clique started slandering him in an attempt to have him ousted from the worksite.

PIETRO TORRIGIANO (1472-1528), sculptor
Famous for having broken Michelangelo's nose, after which he was forced to leave Florence and work in England and then Spain. His violent nature made him a magnet for trouble, and he died in prison.

WHAT WAS MICHELANGELO DOING

SCENARIO 1

The object of adulation and admiration, Michelangelo is a rich gentleman surrounded by dukes and cardinals. He holds the posts of chamberlain (a dignitary with personal responsibilities to the pope) and also of curator of antiquities. He is made a knight of the order of the Golden Spur.

The efficient organization of his studio means that he is able to carry out several commissions simultaneously. He is appointed architect of the works of St. Peter and directs the construction of the new cathedral until his death.

FALSE: The artist here is Raphael (1483-1520), who lived in Rome from 1508 until his death.

SCENARIO 2

While painting the fresco of the *Last Judgment* Michelangelo meets Vittoria Colonna, the marchioness of Pescara. She lives alone, often in a convent, having abandoned society after the death of her husband. She is, however, a poet and holds a salon that attracts a fashionable assembly of notables, literary figures, artists, and clergymen. She enlivens discussions with her remarkable intellect and obvious religious faith. A close friendship grows between the two of them; she is attracted less to Michelangelo the artist than to Michelangelo the man, tormented by the need for faith. In turn, she inspires poems and magnificent drawings. Her death in 1547 drives him "mad with grief."

TRUE: They met in 1536. Michelangelo was sixty-one; Vittoria Colonna, at forty-six, was fifteen years his junior.

IN ROME BETWEEN 1534 AND 1564?

SCENARIO 3

Appointed director and chief engineer in charge of building and maintaining the city's walls, Michelangelo places his prodigious talents as an engineer at the service of Rome. He draws up plans so complex and original that the authorities are reluctant to build them. Disappointed by their distrust and convinced that one of the members of the government has betrayed him, Michelangelo moves to Venice, leaving the city in a turmoil at his departure. His friends prevail upon him to come back, and he returns to his post as chief engineer. The city is thus able to hold out in a ten-month siege.

SCENARIO 4

In his old age, Michelangelo devotes more and more of his time to writing. His correspondence reveals a solitary but generous personality; his poems speak with sensitivity and feeling of physical beauty, love, religious faith, and awareness of death. Most are addressed to Tommaso de' Cavalieri, a young Roman nobleman famous for his beauty who is Michelangelo's friend until his death, and Vittoria Colonna, to whom Michelangelo is drawn by her piety and the fervor of her religious belief.

FALSE: The city was Florence, not Rome, and it was besieged from 1529 to 1530 by the papal troops of Clement VII and the imperial army of Charles V. Michelangelo did indeed serve the city as engineer.

TRUE: Michelangelo's poems were published in 1623 by his grand-nephew. This nephew censored and rewrote some of the poems to Cavalieri because he found them too shocking, a fact that came to light only in 1863.

*Though he has come to
this conclusion earlier,
Copernicus waits until
1543 to make this discovery
known in the sixth volume
of his great work De
Revolutionibus Orbium
Coelestium.* The earth is
no longer the center
around which all planets
revolve and is instead just
one more planet in orbit
around the sun.

1534: BIRTH OF THE CHURCH OF ENGLAND
*Henry VIII, eager to divorce
Catherine of Aragon so he can
marry Anne Boleyn, petitions
Pope Clement VII to have his
marriage invalidated, but the
pope refuses. Henry secretly
marries Anne and is
excommunicated by the pope.
With the support of parliament,
the king creates a national
church separate from the Roman
Catholic Church and becomes the
supreme head of the church and
clergy in England.*

1515: VICTORY OF FRANCIS I AT MARIGNANO
*The French and their Venetian
allies defeat the pope's Swiss
soldiers at Marignano, a small
town near Milan. The bloody
battle leads to peace between the
French and Swiss and also
proves that artillery can be
horribly effective against rows of
infantry.*

THE WO
MICH
IS FAS

OCTOBER 12, 1492: CHRISTOPHER COLUMBUS DISCOVERS AMERICA
*The tireless navigator
and explorer believes he
has discovered a new
route to India (and so
calls all the natives
Indians). America gets
its name from another
Italian navigator,
Amerigo Vespucci, who
explores South America
and proves that it is a
new continent, not part
of Asia.*

56

1517: MARTIN LUTHER NAILS HIS 95 THESES TO THE CHURCH DOOR OF WITTENBERG

The reconstruction of Rome is costly, and the popes get money by selling indulgences, which offer Catholics pardon for sins committed. Martin Luther condemns this practice ("The pope has more need of prayer than money") and others in the theses, or declarations, he nails to the church door. The Protestant revolution has begun, destined to rock the entire century.

1527: THE SACK OF ROME BY IMPERIAL TROOPS

After the Spanish defeat Francis I at Pavia, Pope Clement VII preaches an anti-Spanish policy. An imperial army composed primarily of Protestant German landsknechts *(mercenaries) marches on the Rome and takes the city by storm. The destruction lasts eight days, and the pope flees. The event has major repercussions throughout Catholic Europe.*

1519: CHARLES V IS ELECTED HOLY ROMAN EMPEROR

Charles V possesses vast dominions thanks to his inheritance from the Hapsburgs, from the kings of Castile and Aragon, and from his parents, Philip the Handsome and Joanna the Mad. As emperor, he is the most powerful ruler in Europe and finds himself with plenty of enemies.

O TURNS AS
ANGELO
T WORK

1545 TO 1563: THE COUNCIL OF TRENT

Although Martin Luther has been excommunicated and his views condemned, northern Europe falls under the sway of the Protestant Reformation. Many countries become enmeshed in bloody religious conflicts. Pope Paul III approves the establishment of the order of Jesuits and convenes the Council of Trent in an attempt to strengthen and clarify the Catholic Church's position.

St. Peter's Basilica dates back to a wood-roofed church built in the fourth century during the reign of Constantine. Pope Nicholas V rebuilt part of it in the fifteenth century, and then early in the sixteenth century Julius II decides to rebuild the entire church. He turns to Bramante, who designs a building in the shape of a Greek cross (in which all the arms are of equal length) topped by a dome. Work begins, but in 1514 Bramante dies.

Raphael continues the work until 1520, when Antonio da Sangallo the Younger takes over. He spends seven years building a costly and imposing wooden model of the project. Work moves ahead slowly, for the papacy has little money. When Sangallo dies in 1546, Paul III, an enthusiastic admirer of Michelangelo, asks him to continue the work. By then sixty-one, Michelangelo is reluctant to do so, but in the end he accepts on the condition that, for spiritual rea-

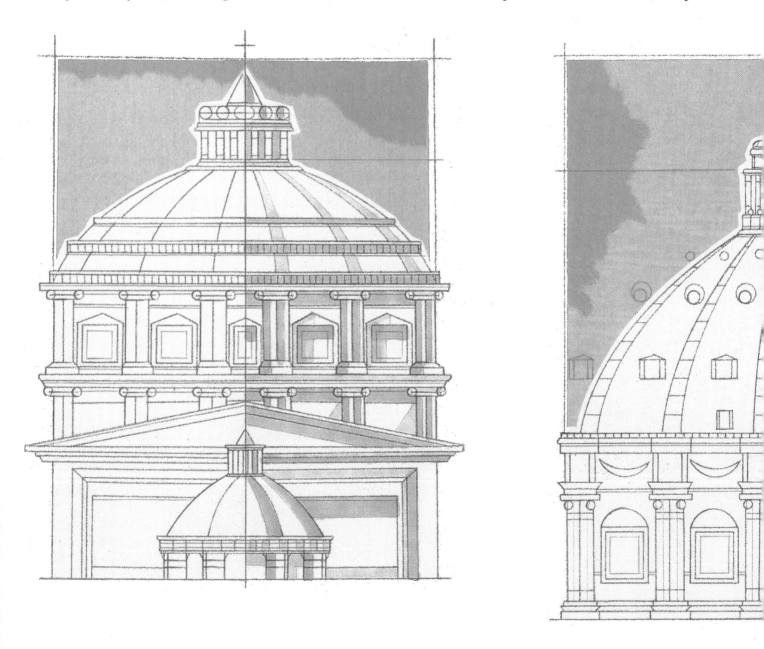

BRAMANTE   YES ☐   NO ☐

MICHELANGELO   YES ☐   NO

HE POPE
ETER'S WOULD YOU CHOOSE?

sons, he not be paid.

Michelangelo had hated Bramante the man, but he honors the man's talent and his design. On the other hand, he is violently critical of Sangallo's model, earning him the hatred of the "Sangallo clique." Fortunately, Paul III, Julius III, and Paul IV all ignore these vicious attacks and confirm Michelangelo's appointment as architect of the new basilica.

Like Bramante, Michelangelo opts for a Greek cross plan. He develops the design for the huge dome and makes a model of it for his workers. Then he dies, and the basilica is not finished until the seventeenth century, based in part on his original plans.

Which plan would you have chosen if you had been pope?

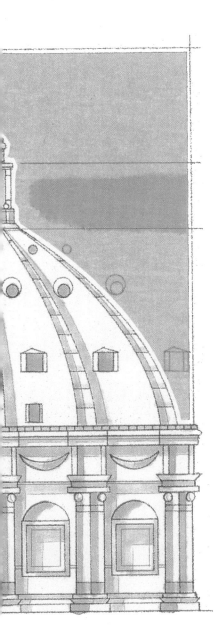

SANGALLO YES ☐ NO ☐

Check the box next to your choice

BEAUTY OF THE BODY

Michelangelo was a deep admirer of the human body and in particular of male beauty. His male nudes are full of passionate feeling, a reflection of the distress of the soul within.

The soul seems to be at war with the body, struggling to free itself from the prison of flesh. Each figure is alone in a world of sorrow.

TORMENT OF THE SOUL

As his religious faith grew, Michelangelo's style changed. His nudes became more massive, though still dynamic and supple. He no longer stressed so much the physical beauty of the body, but rather its inner purity.

His faces betray the violence of these inner struggles: we call this the "terribleness" of Michelangelo. In these faces he shows the pain that we associate with our fear of death and divine judgment.

HERE HE WORKED

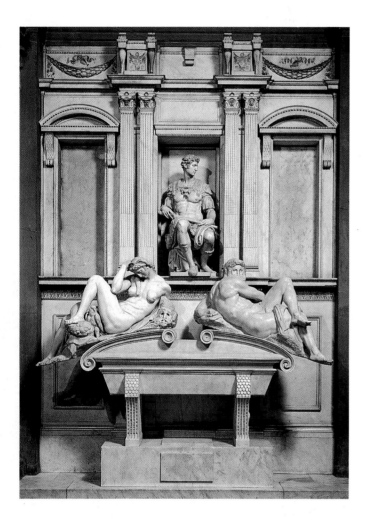

Michelangelo moved to Rome in 1534 and devoted his last years to architecture, poetry, and drawing. Although his strength was declining, he kept up his habit of taking a horse ride every day. On February 14, 1564, he went riding on a rainy, cold day. By the next morning he was feverish and had to take to his bed. He died four days later, surrounded by his friends.

His body, followed by a large crowd, was brought to the Church of the Holy Apostles on February 19. Here, the pope announced that a tomb would be built for him in St. Peter's.

But Michelangelo had wanted to be buried in his homeland, the city of Florence, and to respect this wish his nephew Leonardo spirited the body away, "disguised as a piece of merchandise," as Vasari reports.

The convoy arrived in Florence on March 10. The coffin was displayed before burial in the Church of Santa Croce, where Michelangelo's ancestors were interred. Painters, sculptors, and architects assembled around the coffin in silent mourning.

On July 14, an official memorial service was given, organized by the members of the Florentine Academy for the Arts. Michelangelo was the first artist to be honored in this way.

Grand Duke Cosimo de' Medici donated the marble for a monument to Michelangelo to be built, Giorgio Vasari designed it, and it was sculpted by Battista Lorenzi. Its statues, representing Painting, Sculpture, and Architecture, mourn the death of the "divine" Michelangelo.

Michelangelo, tomb of Giuliano de' Medici, duke of Nemours, 1520-34, Church of San Lorenzo, Florence

Michelangelo, tomb of Lorenzo di Piero de' Medici, duke of Urbino, 1520-34, Church of San Lorenzo, Florence

These tombs were placed in the New Sacristy of the Church of San Lorenzo, known as the Medici Chapel, which Michelangelo completed in 1534. They are famous for their allegorical representations of Day and Night and Dawn and Dusk, the bodies of which powerfully express human anguish at the inevitability of death.

Giorgio Vasari, ▶ tomb of Michelangelo, 1564-68, Church of Santa Croce, Florence

HERE HE RESTS

INDEX

BOOKS FOR FURTHER READING

Beckett, Sister Wendy, and Wright, Patricia. *The Story of Painting: The Essential Guide to the History of Western Art*. New York: Dorling Kindersley, 1995.

Goldsheider, Ludwig. *Michelangelo: Paintings, Sculpture, Architecture*. San Francisco: Chronicle Books, 1995.

Hager, Serafina, ed. *Leonardo, Michelangelo, and Raphael: In Renaissance Florence, 1500-1508*. Washington, D.C.: Georgetown University Press, 1992.

Hartt, Frederick. *Michelangelo*. Masters of Art series. New York: Harry N. Abrams, 1984.

Lace, William W. *Michelangelo*. San Diego: Lucent Books, 1993.

Lebot, Mark. *Michelangelo*. New York: Crown, 1992.

McLanathan, Richard. *Michelangelo*. New York: Harry N. Abrams, 1993.

Michelangelo Buonarroti. *The Complete Poetry of Michelangelo*. Edited and trans. by Sidney Alexander. Columbus: Ohio State University Press, 1991.

———. *Life Drawings*. New York: Dover, 1990.

———. *Life, Letters, and Poetry*. Edited by George Bull. Oxford and New York: Oxford University Press, 1987.

———. *Michelangelo: A Record of His Life as Told in His Own Letters and Papers*. Trans. by Robert W. Carden. New York: Gordon Press Publishers, 1976.

Murray, Linda and Peter. *Art of the Renaissance*. New York: Thames and Hudson, 1963.

Pietrangeli, Carlo, et al. *The Sistine Chapel: The Art, the History, and the Restoration*. New York: Random House, 1986.

Rabb, Theodore K. *Renaissance Lives: Portraits of an Age*. New York: Pantheon, 1993.

Stone, Irving. *The Agony and the Ecstasy*. New York: Dutton, 1987.

Tolnay, Charles de. *Michelangelo*. 5 vols. Princeton: Princeton University Press, 1943-60.

Vasari, Giorgio. *Lives of the Artists*. Edited and trans. by Julia C. and Peter Bondadella. Oxford and New York: Oxford University Press, 1991.

ILLUSTRATIONS

PHOTOGRAPHS

PHOTO CREDITS